it is always night

by tana

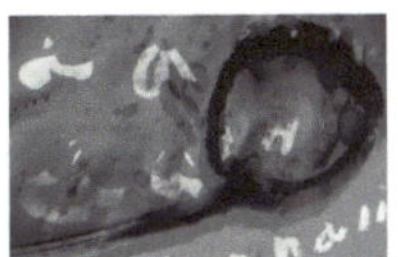

The Dandelion Planet

P.O. Box 18, Lions Bay

V0N 2E0, BC, Canada

ISBN hardcover: 978-0-9858153-2-5

ISBN paperback: 978-0-9858153-3-2

Poetry, Women studies

Library of Congress Control Number:2012956049

Also available as an EBOOK.

Cover photo and illustrations by tana.

to guillermo

1.

white

frozen

vanishing

2.

it gleams

the dark

the ice

3.

blind

blazing

into the black

4.

a brief

brightening

my eye blinks

5.

i am an eye

a planet

s e e i n g

6.

bits of brown

green over a gray

blurry roundness

7.

i absorb light

look

search

8.

always

rushing away

from *now*

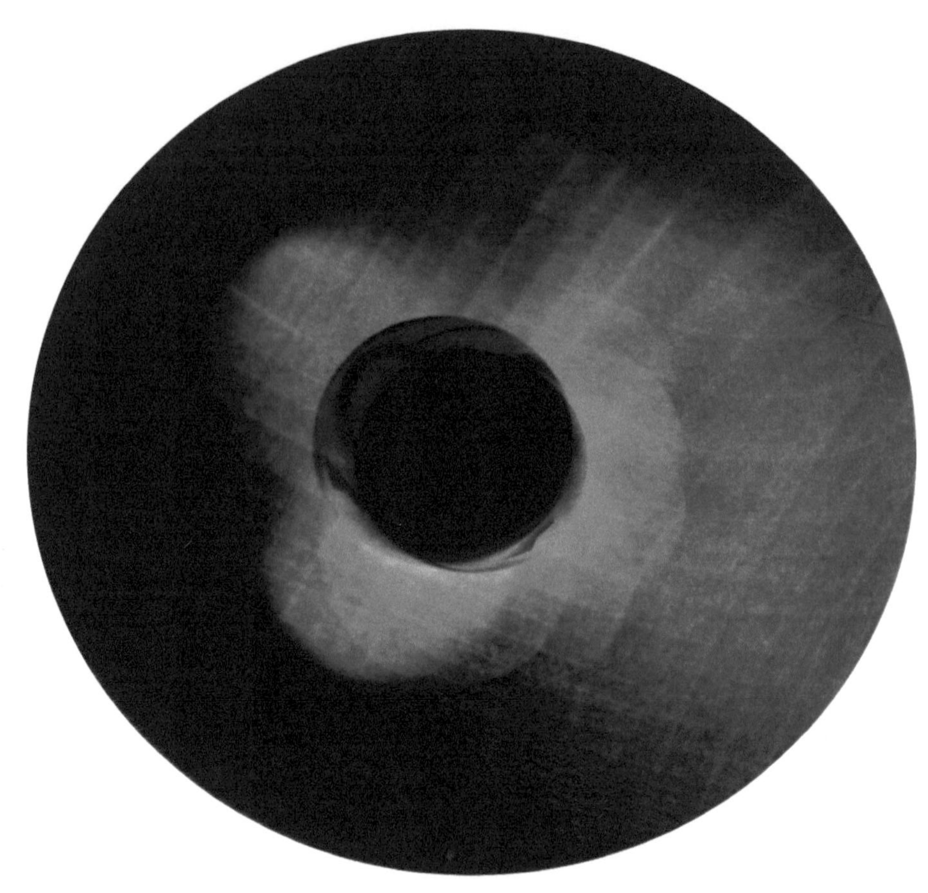

9.

the s t r e t c h e d

argent comet

distracts me

10.

its utter loneliness

its blind pupil

its s l o w passing

11.

arms spread out

carrying light

as it recedes

12.

then flatness

i turn my glance

to far apart bodies

13.

scattered

long lasting

distances

14.

space holds me

still i won't

look down

15.

and

down is

everywhere

16.

cannot help

but look

      i could

17.

fall

yet light flits by

      i f o l l o w

18.

light   so rare

journeys

always

19.

not me

not much

not really

20.

remote

solid

i hide

21.

a barren surface

no atmosphere

    i count orbits

22.

must have lost

count

    time

23.

i do try again

to count

yet time won't

24.

won't come back

i am afraid *back* is

wrong too

25.

space

curves

    undulates

26.

as i watch

i see

her

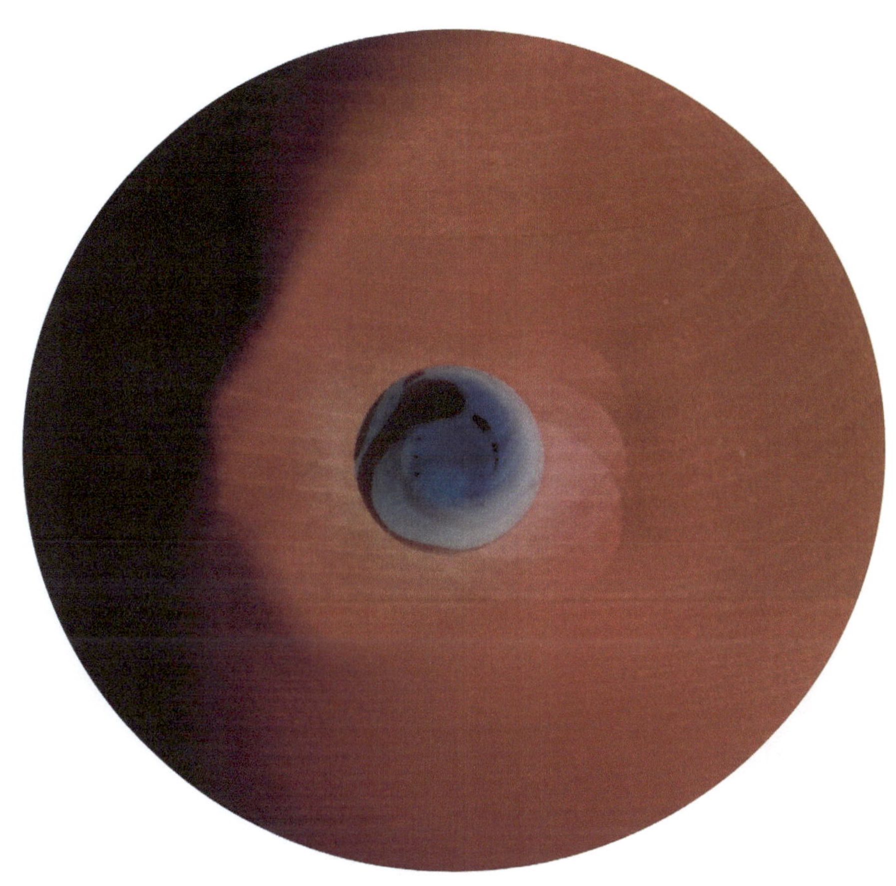

27.

a pupil

a planet

gazing out

28.

she is *jane*

a redblue planet

in the void

29.

opaque

as the dark

   and red

30.

she looks

down

at a path

31.

so far she has not

been swallowed

she half wants

32.

half wants

it

it being gravity

33.

gravity

an end

i see

34.

the path

is also

a mouth

35.

two white dwarves

shine close

to its bending

36.

two eyes

a face

a distorted face

37.

a black wide

tongueless mouth

        too close

38.

restless

i pretend not to see

b u t   i   d o

39.

hardly any space

hardly any time   left

is that what *sadness* is

40.

squeeze*ness*

being

too late

41.

so much

so dizzy

rotation keeps me

42.

from

f

a

l

l

i

n

g

43.

a pull

with

eyes

44.

hellium

filamentsthickdust

blur my sight

45.

n

o

t

h

i

n

g

left

46.

nonluminous clouds

behindaroundbehindme

        i stare blank

47.

massive

not wanted

bleak

48.

i did not

mean to look

that way

49.

uncomfortably close

i   must   orbit

somewhere else

50.

i observe jane

fragile

unaware

51.

i hold her

with

my eye

52.

far into the night

ice melts

    a kind of crying

53.

curled

into herself

round

54.

a sudden fear

oppresses me

bursting void

55.

seems

to touch her with

indifference

56.

a depth

with mouths

eyes

57.

lifeless

i notice

a brown jade planet

58.

he stares back

    i don't think

      he can see me

59.

must be

looking at these

dusty clouds

60.

i am just

a dot

in time

61.

i

hide

i hide

62.

planets

around me

   long gone

63.

space

and time

at odds

64.

surely

time needs s p a c e

and yet

65.

maybe not

   all that staring

   and not enough

66.

orbiting

i know i must

i must

67.

still

i see

one of the eyes

68.

in the hungry face

sucking

jane's

69.

glow

and

i   f o r g e t

70.

sheistrappedinamber

cannot keep looking

and counting

71.

i would orbit

more willingly

if   i   could

72.

a sudden somnolence

slightly

falling

73.

eyes

do

sleep

74.

through

the endless

continuous

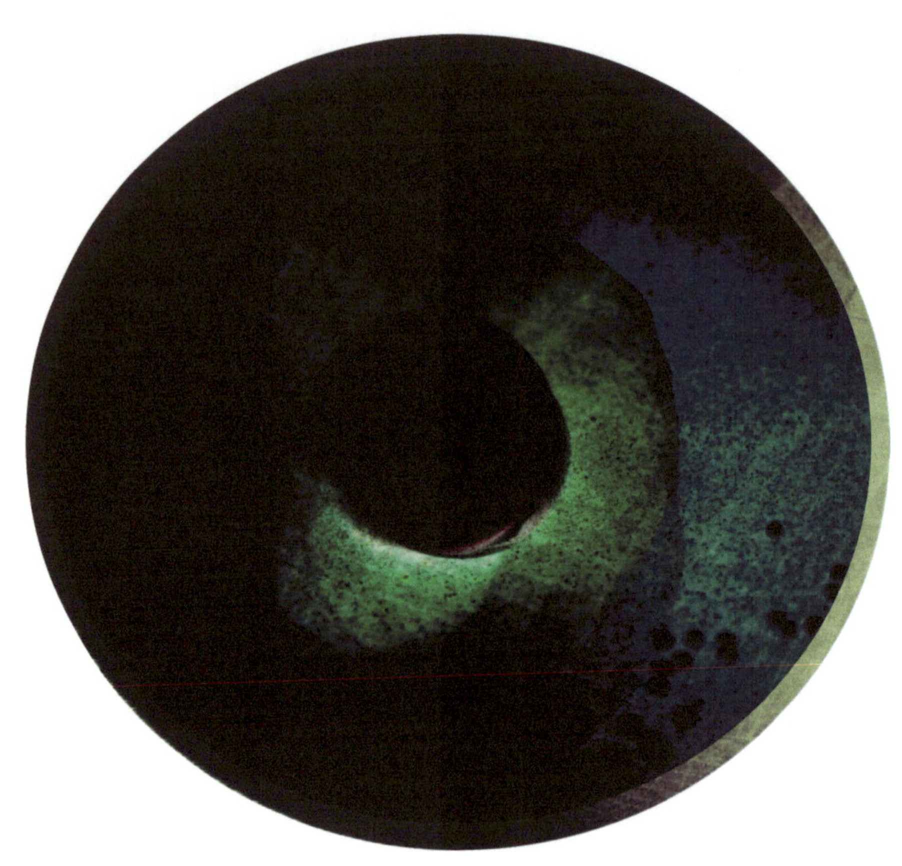

75.

n *i* g h t

it is time

not space

76.

what

i search for

      lost

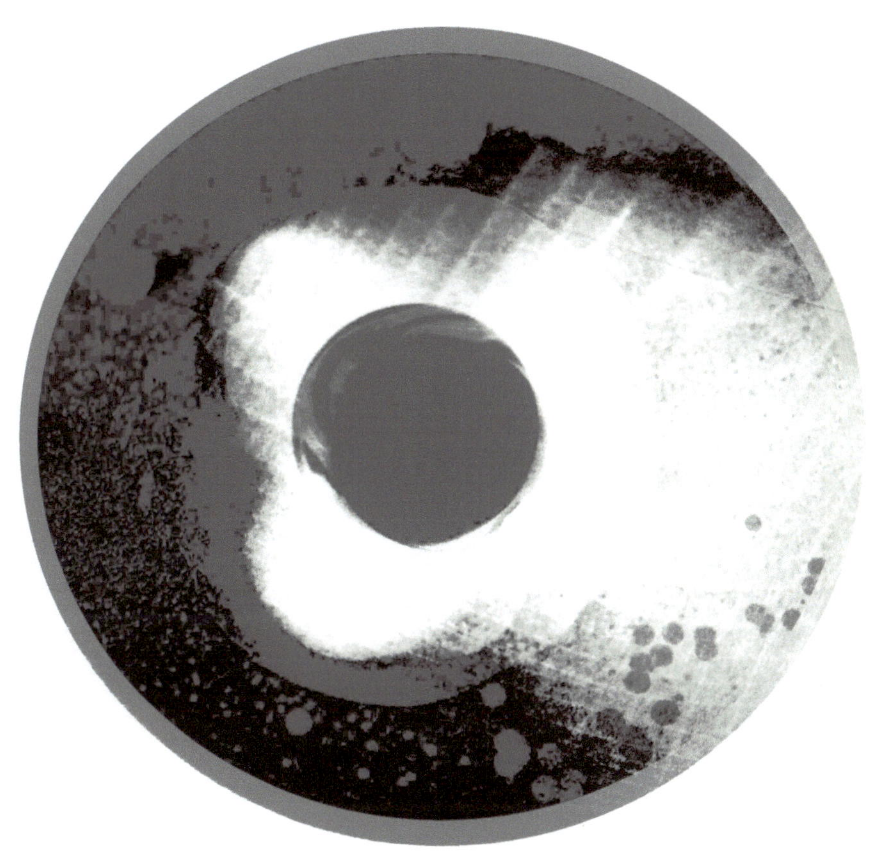

77.

    a fleeting

ephemeral gauze

blowing

78.

a mauve milky

blowing velvet

with me inside

79.

close though

a neutron star

    waits

80.

dead

spinning

insistent

81.

blinking   *am i*

a colorless *hiding*

light   *from her?*

82.

furiously *i*

into my   *want her*

eye   *to stop*

83.

she goes

leaving me

half blind

84.

a white dream

so much light then

an abrupt fall

85.

m a r bles

p l a nets

d   all

r   a

o   t

p   once

86.

emptiness

vacuum

i wake up

87.

the

loneliness

of the eye

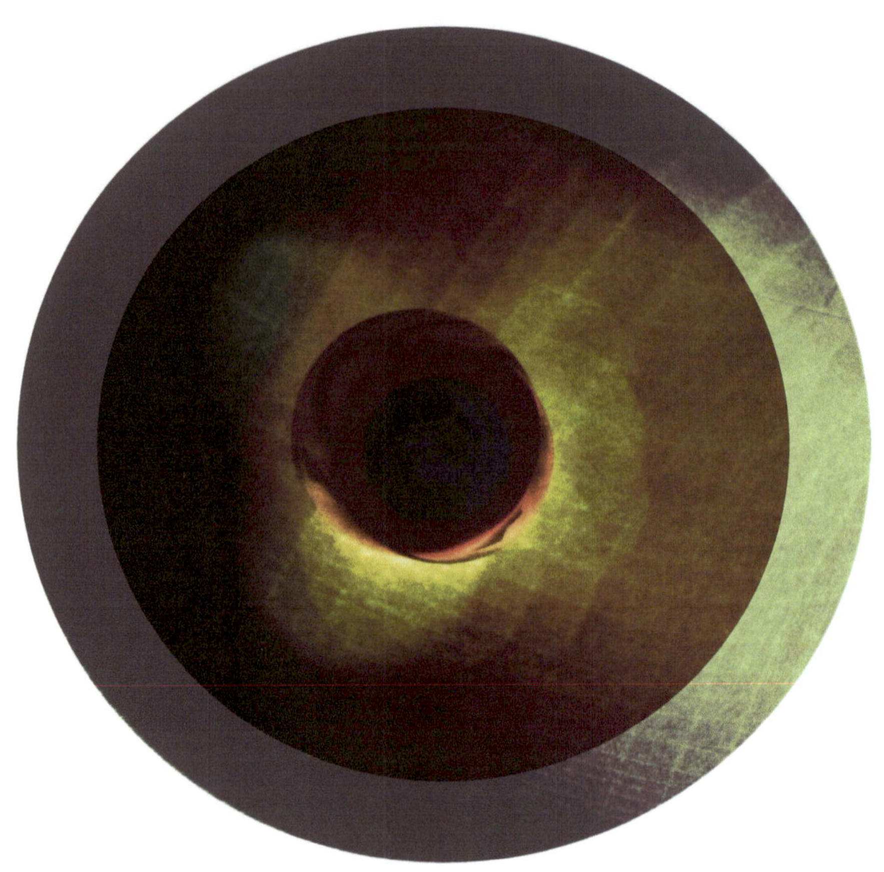

88.

light**less**

   far

unnoticed

89.

jane's pupil

grows a bit

she just saw me

90.

i sight

her eye says

tana

91.

i can see you

i feel her

close

92.

i can see you too

silence

flatness

93.

i keep

looking

an eye

94.

within an eye

cuts

distance

95.

pain

a sharp

burning strain

96.

it is   her eye

she is   crying fire

she is   in flames

97.

i observe with horror

the devouring

eye

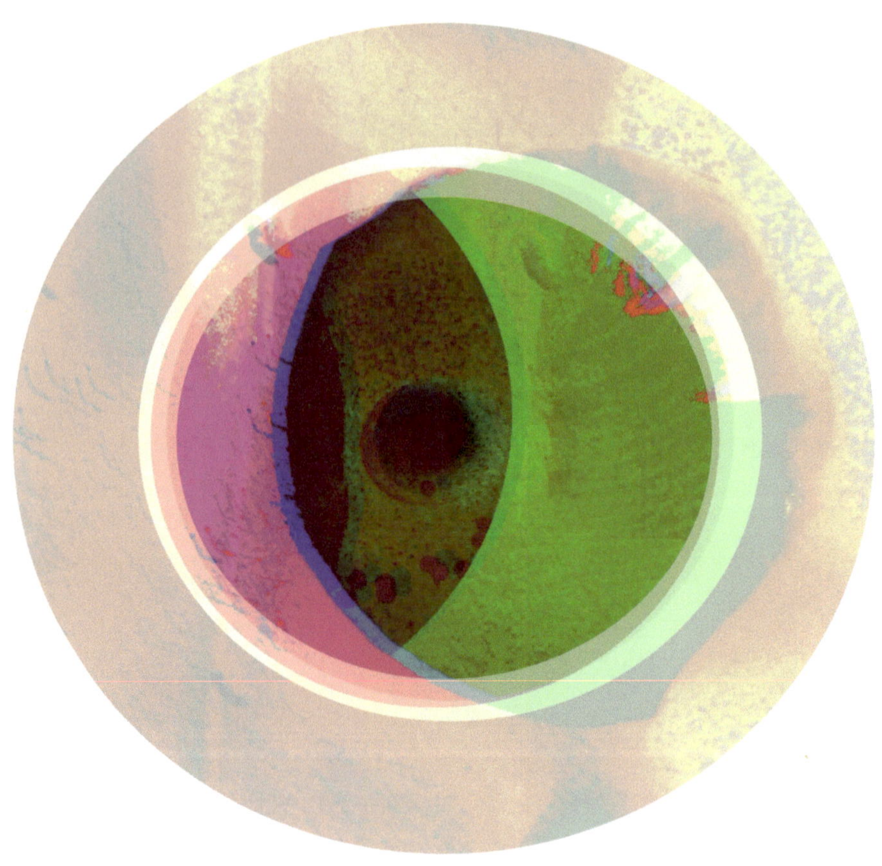

98.

and horror

is   a

hole

99.

i must avoid depth

search for a point

in the transparent far

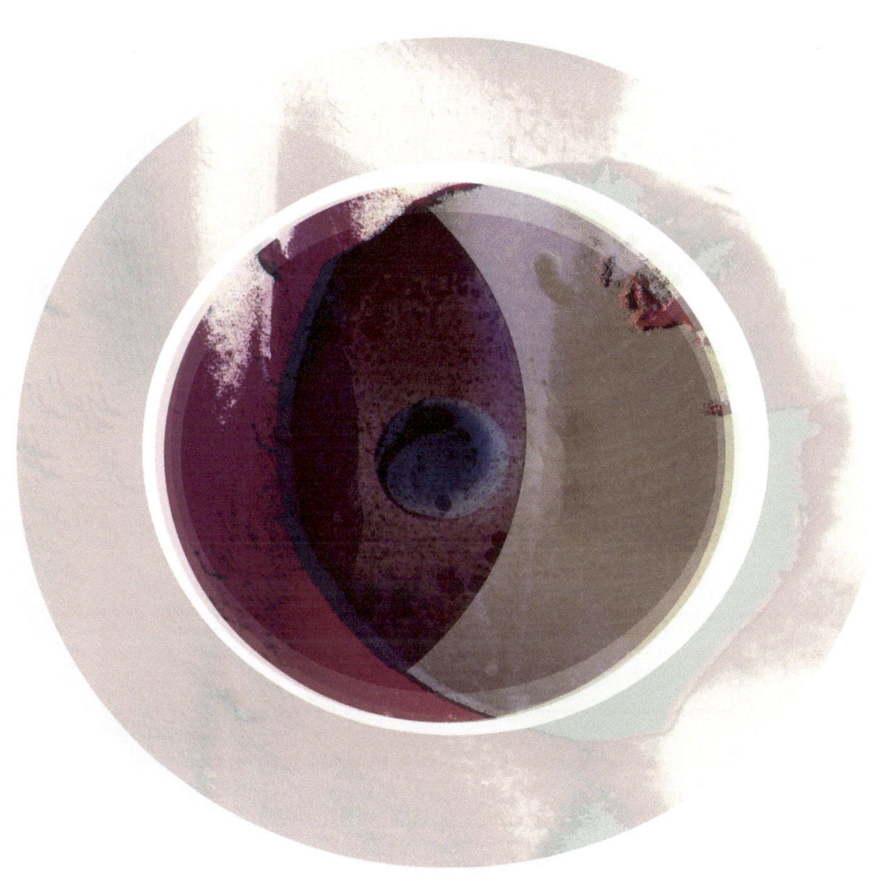

100.

i must

i must

take care to count

101.

unless

i want

to fall

102.

distance

fills me

with distance

103.

and

despair

    i wanted to help

104.

i simply

cannot hold

anything with my eye

105.

brown

and green

and grey no more

106.

won't be a planet

anymore

the dizziness of it

107.

flames die out

in the never ending

night

108.

her planet

    just

an ashy shell

109.

translucent

delicate

    a dandelion

110.

a wish

    won't blow it

but keep it

111.

wish or not

makes

    no difference

112.

slowly she slides

down

the black hole

113.

i turn

i stare at dust around

mad

114.

time

has no meaning

unless it is *now*

115.

so it's now

i must do it

    trembling

116.

with comet's

candle light still

in my pupil

117.

i explore dust

its gloomy

matter

118.

a stagnant gas

minute fibers

sparkling filaments

119.

loose threads

disperse

r u b b l e

120.

i see

destr u   c   t   i   o   n

i see

121.

nothing

     because

nothing is left

122.

but me and

a path

in the darkness

123.

we stand

so close

     the clouds and i

124.

to the edge

i want nothing

but to   fall

125.

gravity

i close my eye

give in to **verti g o**

126.

d

o

w

n

i

r o l l

127.

<pre>
d   t   e   h
o   h   v   o
w   e   n   r
n   t   i
                        z o n
</pre>

128.

a sphere

a **ball**

   blue and beautiful

129.

    and it wants *me*

i follow

in the black

130.

so heavy

i cannot see

    it waits for me

131.

rolling

rolling smoothly

a child's ball

132.

unconcerned

blackness folds

unfolds

133.

we go round

and round

playfully

134.

the blue ball

becomes an eye

round and empty

135.

it is a way

through

    i am out

136.

very awake and

blind just a

cluster of vibrations

137.

i hardly

warp

space

138.

subtle

weightless

passing

139.

energy

crosses

incessantly

140.

i don't mind

the rippling

the silky currents

141.

i would not want

to be more

yet

142.

a pressure

a tightness

   an advancing

143.

force

pushes me

hard

144.

an enormous hefty

winding current

a river

145.

flowing **murky**

tarni**shed** **energy**

conside**rs** me

146.

faintest

spinning

stops

147.

it is scarier

than the face

i won't

148.

i won't be a river

a sullen hostile

drowning substance

149.

it dives again

into the night

nooooooooooooo

150.

pulling

mealongwith

itstwistytail

151.

deeper into an

unknown tide

all i want is

152.

to see

to cry

i need an eye

153.

river c u t s

it leaves

wounds behind

154.

a blueberry density

bending

as it passes by

155.

some matter stops

this incessant hurting

   i guess its volume

156.

its shape

   a wing

   a flapping wing

157.

a flying

nebula

a giant butterfly

158.

my dead star

   i cannot see still

it must be mauve

159.

dead stars grow

glittery wings

i am floating in time

160.

jane

my wish came true

it's my butterfly

161.

she flies through me

to and fro

i am not just

162.

a loose thread

a massless vibration

i am more

163.

i glow

   no one is left

i whisper

164.

just me

just me

   do not leave me

165.

she fades though

time's fabric won't

hold for long

166.

i understand

no   i   don't

riverdivesoncemore

167.

along

i wander

the night

168.

true i cannot really

tell but

planets seem sleepy

169.

their hazy eyes

dreamy not seeing

i want to cry

170.

i sink

it is a way of crying

to sink

171.

river slithers

away

its tail

172.

loses me

i slowly wane into

the massless ocean

173.

i cry deep

each tiny lingering

string cries deep

174.

not seeing

not expecting

a tentacle

175.

a wormhole

that sucks me in

compressedddddd

176.

terribly squeezed

into a **flat** sadness

then a pause

177.

pressure

dimensions shrink

then abruptly blow

178.

into a balloon

i fill it

i am the wormhole

179.

inside me

a me so big

some

180.

cornered

marbles **and**

a worn mask

181.

oh no *not the face*

it grins

it's deformed

182.

my sadness fills me

my planets

my black hole

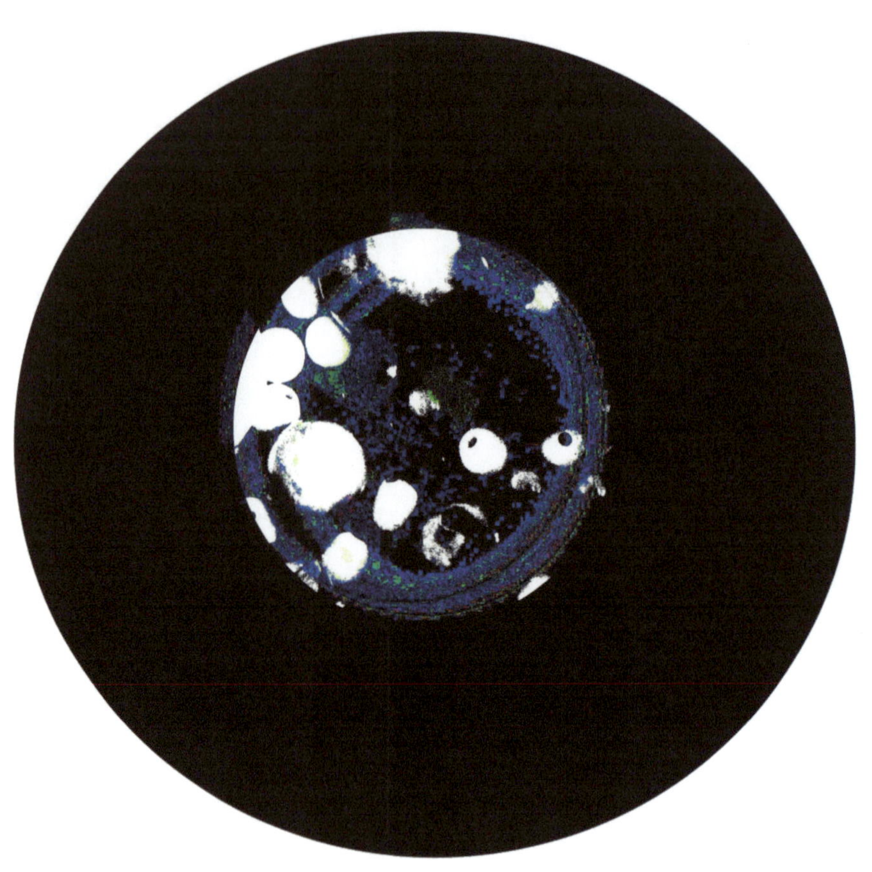

183.

are *back*

there is

no now

184.

just

only

back

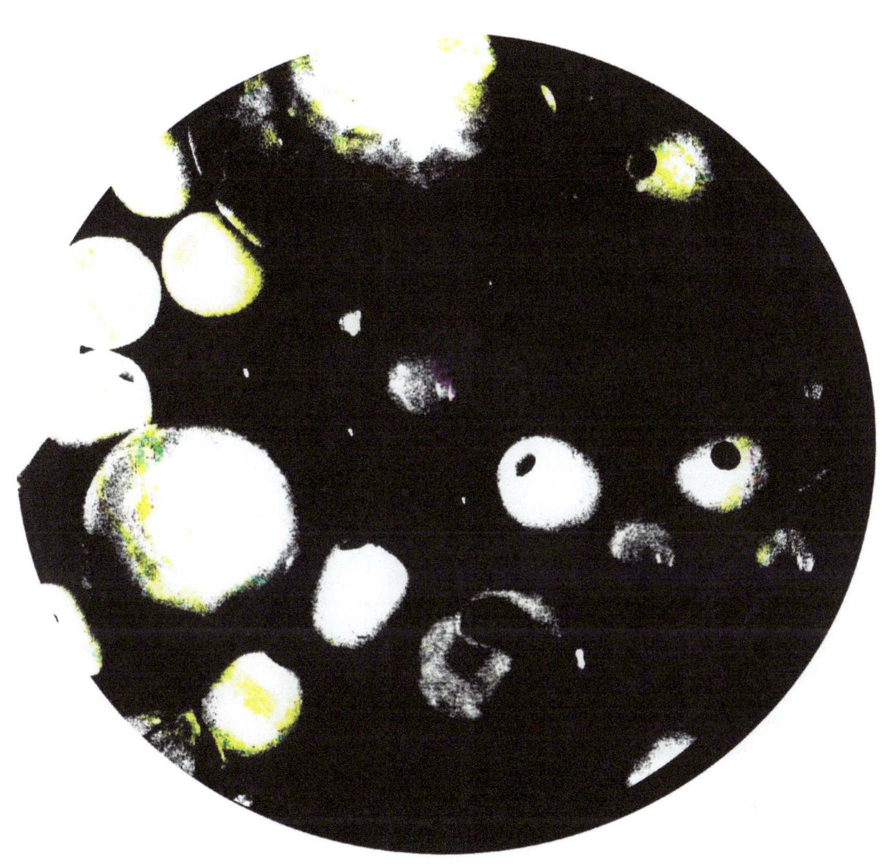

185.

trapped

swollen

dizzy

186.

and too big

    stuck

a nightmare

187.

still a wormhole

is a way

out

188.

i must wake up

i must find

an opening

189.

wake up tana

wallsexpandcontract

i push

190.

push hard

againandagain

my marbles roll

191.

backandforth

my long gone planets

sorry

192.

i must get out

get through

the tiniest hole

193.

Squeezedoncemore

i lose size   b u r s t

i pop out of myse l f

194.

a torn ragged

one dimensional

thread

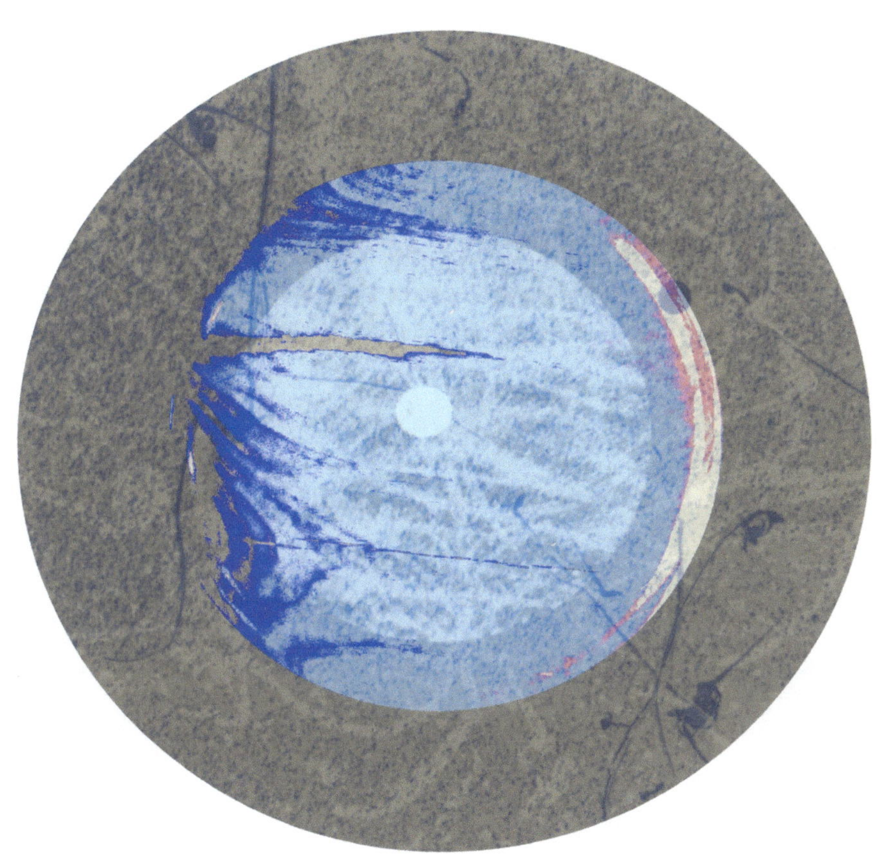

195.

ejected with force

yet

i won't cry

196.

astray

loose

half awake

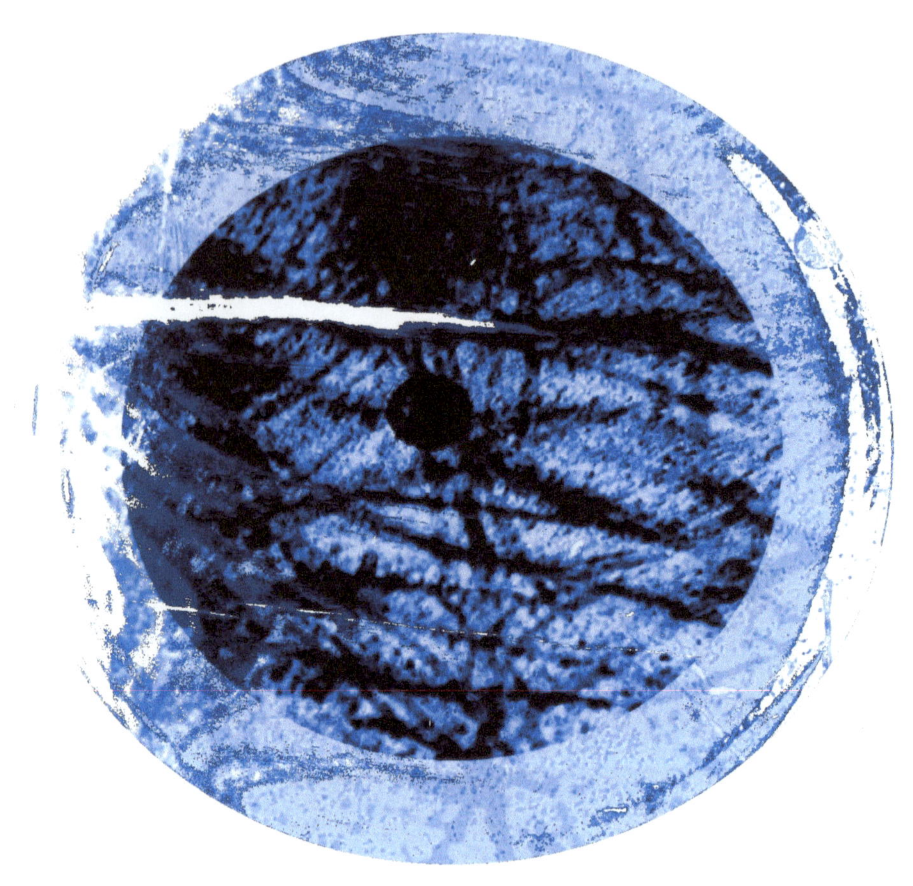

197.

i am being touched

space's fabric

touches me

198.

it is sewing me

into itself slowly

within without

199.

imperceptibly

i am a waving fabric

an evanescent blanket

200.

planets curve me

i feel the weight

the rhythm

201.

the music

i touch them

carefully

202.

knowing

they fear

down

203.

down is nothing

but   distance

plus   time

204.

anxiously i ponder

over the fabric

worry about its texture

205.

itsholesitsknots

i begin to shiver

close   a jane planet

206.

a planet

rolled up so

it won't

207.

fall

updownleftright

fall **inside**

208.

not again

i feel so cold

i am turning into ice

209.

jane

do not look

d

o

w

n

210.

search for a point

i am here

i am close

211.

shaking

i feel the mouth

open wide**wider**

212.

i feel its throat

and *jane* small

as candy

213.

red and white

sliding

into a belly

214.

helium comes out

a spiraling

flare of radiation

215.

adrynarrowtongue

l o n g

winding around

216.

and around

till it's

gone

217.

flat

once more

cold

218.

i am cold

solid cold

ice cold

219.

fabric's stitches

unfasten around me

ice weights

220.

spherical

and solid

i become a comet

221.

drifting

merely

crossing

222.

symmetry repeats

and conceals

more symmetry

223.

another jane

and another jane

a maze

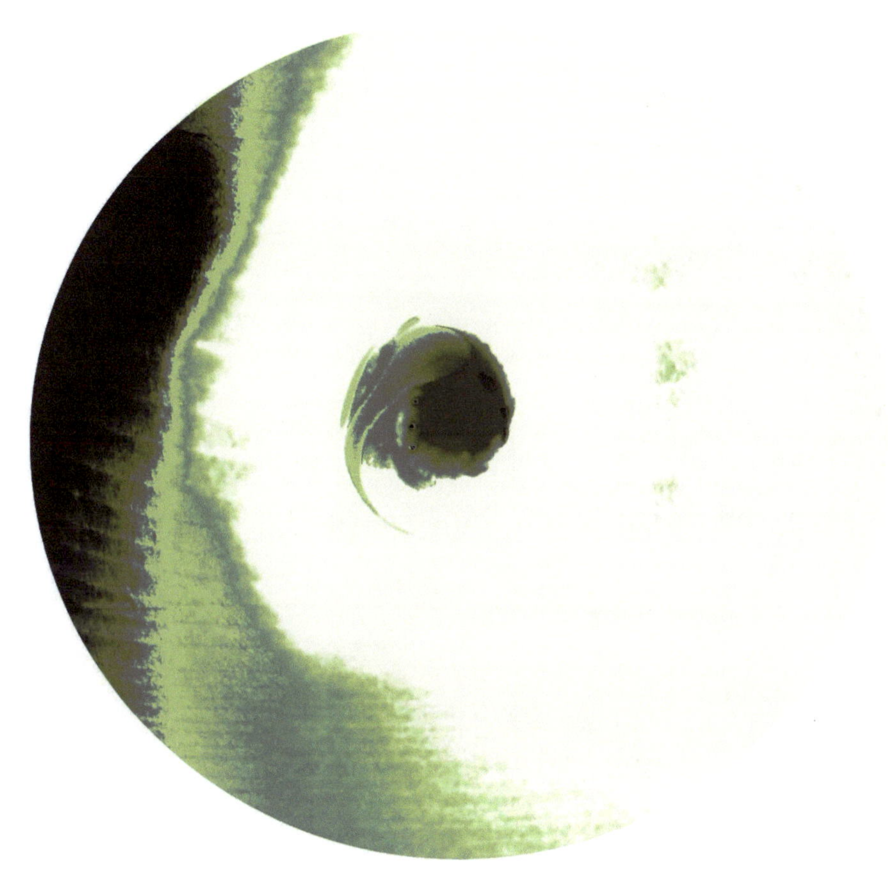

224.

i reflect light

carry it

with my long arms

225.

my white pupil

not b l i n d

sees sadness

226.

i said i wouldn't

but i cry

and melt

227.

a kind of crying

my tears

glow in the night

228.

as i finally

fully

see

229.

*time fills **distance***

layers and layers

of down

230.

light

long ago light

needs time

231.

reaches

when is not

there

232.

seen

only too

late

233.

i am

    no more

    a bright

234.

    blazing

    candle

i go along

235.

making paths

across

spacetime

236.

    i know

i was never

an eye

237.

i was never eaten

never squeezed

no it did not

238.

did not really

happened

but i feel

239.

it did

in a way

it all did

240.

    i know

i do

i know

241.

still i feel

it is always

always night

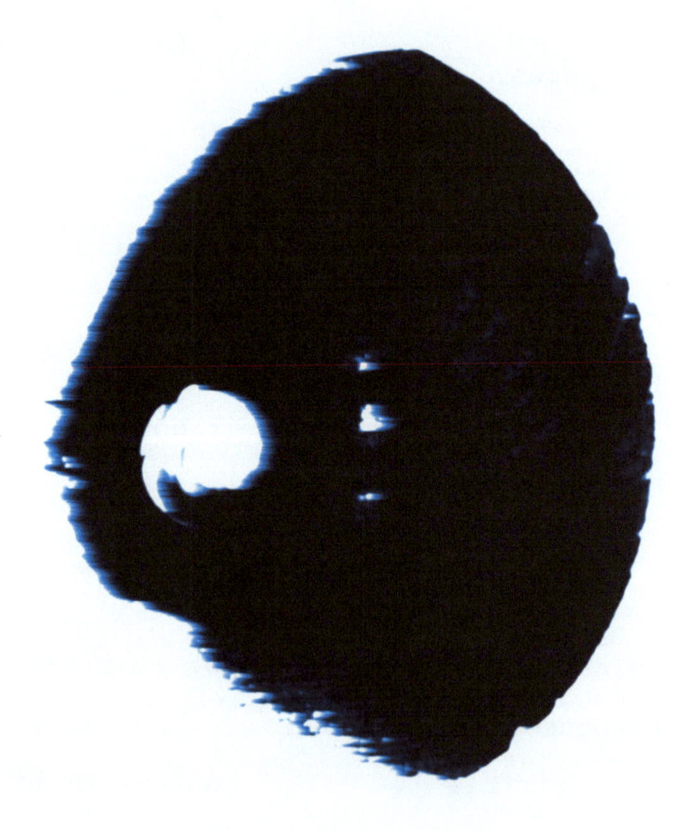